To all dog lovers and their friends

A dog's life is simple

A dog lives in the moment

Nor cares about the past, nor panics about the future

A dog's love is unquestioning

And will stay with you even if you think you are alone

A dog will eat each meal like it's the last

And live each day as if it's the first

A dog's life intertwined with yours
Will leave paw prints on your heart
And more importantly
If followed closely
The wisdom of a dog........

........Will guide you to happiness

The first step is often the hardest

Hold a pure vision in your heart of what you want and it will come to you

Know when to rest

Cherish your freedom

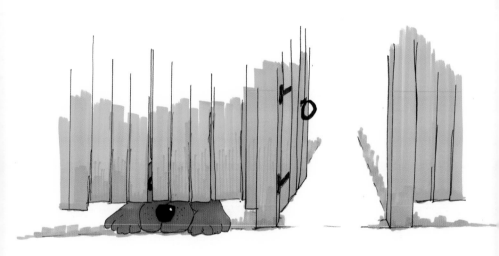

The right way is often the easiest

Share the gifts you have been given

Stop and smell the flowers

If you have to stop and think about walking up a path, it's the wrong path

The quieter you are the more you will hear

Love unconditionally

*Do not believe everything your eyes
are telling you*

Only in silence will you hear your true voice

Faithfulness is the perfect relationship

Learn from your last mistake

*Don't be sad to say goodbye.
A farewell is needed before you can
say 'Hello' again*

Let go. It's often as simple as that

It's only when the journey gets hard
that you discover true friendship

If you stay focused on one tree you won't see the whole forest

You will know a true friend when
you meet them

Take delight in the small things

Take time to feel the wind in your ears

Take time to listen to the ones you love the most

I'm here because I'd rather be with you than anyone else in the world

We are never alone when we look to the stars

Feel the earth beneath your paws

Every end is a beginning

Woof